Nicaragua

by Sweetie Peason

Consultant: Marjorie Faulstich Orellana, PhD
Professor of Urban Schooling
University of California, Los Angeles

BEARPORT
PUBLISHING

New York, New York

Credits

Cover, © Kanokratnok/Shutterstock and © Hogan Imaging/Shutterstock; TOC, © Riderfoot/Shutterstock; 4, © Svetlana Bykova/Alamy; 5T, © Pete Niesen Select Images/Alamy; 5B, © elnavegante/Shutterstock; 7, © Mario Gyß/Alamy; 8–9, © DavorLovincic/iStock; 10T, © Rafal Cichawa/Shutterstock; 10B, © Wolfgang Diederich/imageBROKER; 11, © New York Public Library/Science Source; 12L, Public Domain; 12–13, © Mario Lopez/Epa/REX/Shutterstock; 14–15, © dimarik/iStock; 15R, © rj lerich/Shutterstock; 16T, © Joel Carlliet/iStock; 16B, © Vergani Fotografia/Shutterstock; 17, © Sjors737/Dreamstime; 18T, © Venemama/Dreamstime; 18B, © Ton Koene/VWPics/Redux Pictures; 19L, © Barry Lewis/Alamy; 19R, © David Coleman/Alamy; 20, © AS Food Studio/Shutterstock; 21, © Ildi Papp/Shutterstock; 22–23, © Leroy Francis/Hemis/Alamy; 23R, © Icon Sports Media 702/Newscom; 24, © Leroy Francis/Hemis/Alamy; 25T, © kungverylucky/Shutterstock; 25M, © Edwin Butler/Shutterstock; 25B, © Travel Stock/Shutterstock; 26–27, © Simon Dannhauer/Shutterstock; 27R, © Valerii Shanin/Alamy; 28L, © Esteban Felix/AP Images; 28R, © Nikada/iStock; 29, © Oswaldo Rivas/Reuters; 30T, © Siempreverde22/Dreamstime and © Brendan Berkley/Public Domain; 30B, © charles taylor/Shutterstock; 31 (T to B), © riderfoot/iStock, © Matyas Rehak/Shutterstock, © MTCcurado/iStock, © Wasan Ritthawon/Shutterstock, © Riderfoot/Shutterstock, and © Terry Honeycutt/Shutterstock; 32, © Jim Pruitt/Shutterstock.

Publisher: Kenn Goin
Senior Editor: Joyce Tavolacci
Creative Director: Spencer Brinker
Design: Debrah Kaiser
Photo Researcher: Thomas Persano

Library of Congress Cataloging-in-Publication Data

Names: Peason, Sweetie, author.
Title: Nicaragua / by Sweetie Peason.
Description: New York, New York : Bearport Publishing, 2019. | Series:
    Countries we come from | Includes bibliographical references and index.
Identifiers: LCCN 2018009258 (print) | LCCN 2018009560 (ebook) |
    ISBN 9781684027323 (ebook) | ISBN 9781684026869 (library)
Subjects: LCSH: Nicaragua—Juvenile literature.
Classification: LCC F1523.2 (ebook) | LCC F1523.2 .P43 2019 (print) |
    DDC 972.85—dc23
LC record available at https://lccn.loc.gov/2018009258

For more information, write to Bearport Publishing Company, Inc., 45 West 21st Street, Suite 3B, New York, New York 10010. Printed in the United States of America.

10 9 8 7 6 5 4 3 2 1

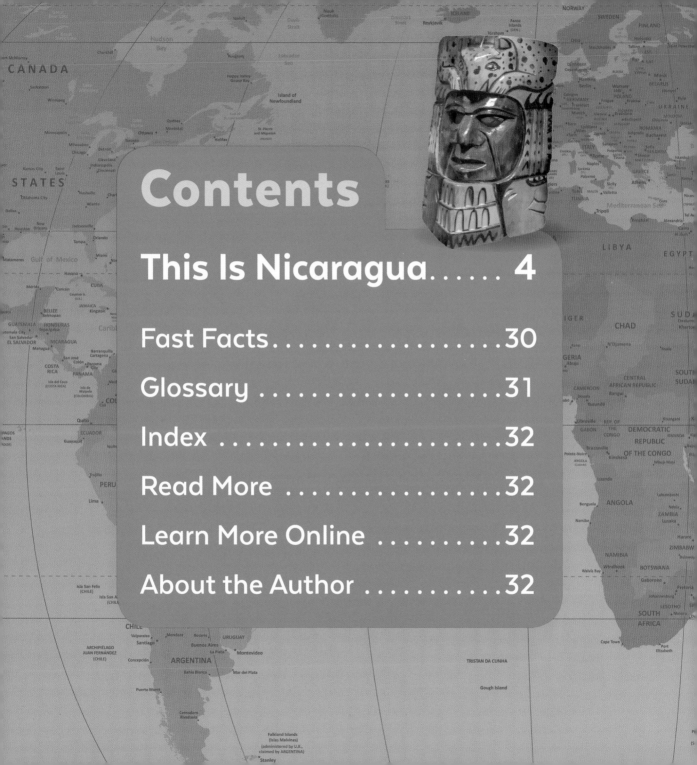

Contents

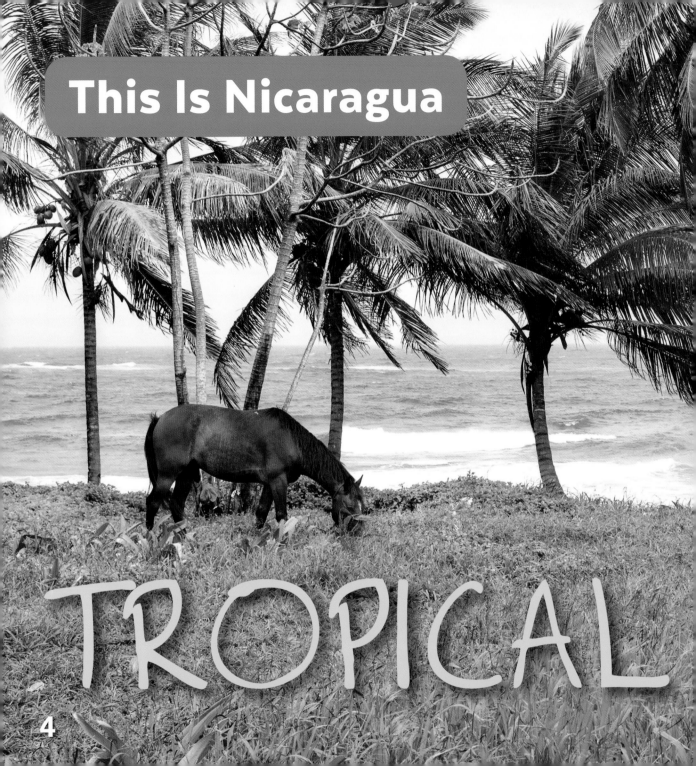

TROPICAL

VOLCANIC

Dazzling

Nicaragua is the largest country in Central America.

It's almost as big as New York.

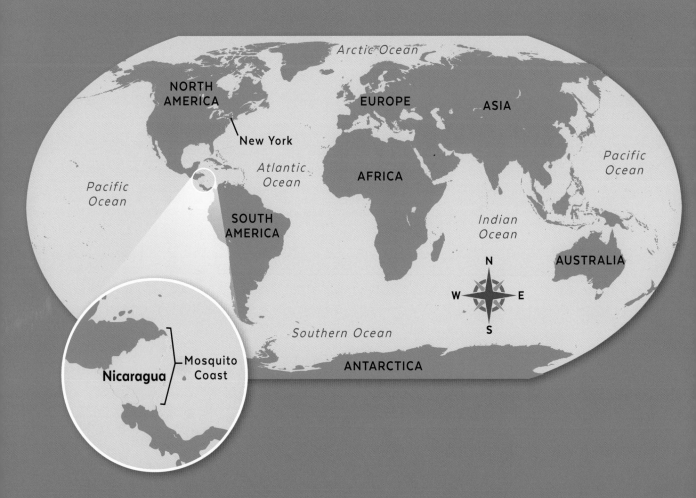

Over 6 million people call Nicaragua home.

7

Nicaragua is known as the "land of lakes and **volcanoes**."

High in Nicaragua's mountains are cloud forests. There, clouds often cover the trees.

The country also has flat, grassy areas and **lush** rain forests.

For thousands of years, people have lived in Nicaragua.

This rock was carved over 3,000 years ago!

The eastern coast of Nicaragua is called the Mosquito Coast. It's named after the Miskito, or Mosquito, people.

In the 1500s, Spain took over the western part of the country.

During the 1600s, the British ruled the Mosquito Coast on the east.

Nicaragua became free from Spanish rule in 1821.

In 1895, the British gave up their control of the Mosquito Coast.

Nicaraguans celebrate their freedom on September 15.

Pirates once roamed the Mosquito Coast.

Managua is Nicaragua's **capital** and biggest city.

It's home to almost one million people.

14

León is Nicaragua's second-largest city.

The main language in Nicaragua is Spanish.

This is how you say *market*:

Mercado
(mehr-KA-doh)

This is how you say *beans*:

Frijoles
(free-HOH-layz)

English creole and Miskito are also spoken in Nicaragua.

Most people in Nicaragua are Roman Catholic.

They worship in big **cathedrals** and small churches.

La Purísima is a major holiday. It celebrates the mother of Jesus. Children go from house to house, asking for treats.

What's on the menu?

A famous Nicaraguan dish is *gallo pinto* (GAH-yo PIN-toh).

It includes rice, beans, and spices.

Gallo pinto means "spotted rooster." Why? The dish looks like a rooster's speckled feathers!

Tostones are fried plantains. Plantains are similar to bananas. They're part of many meals.

21

Time to play ball!

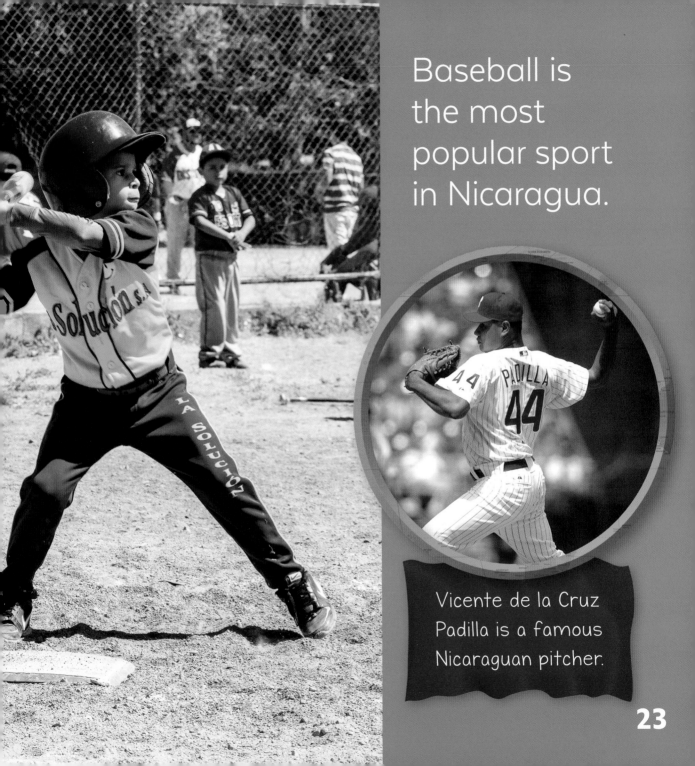

Baseball is the most popular sport in Nicaragua.

Vicente de la Cruz Padilla is a famous Nicaraguan pitcher.

23

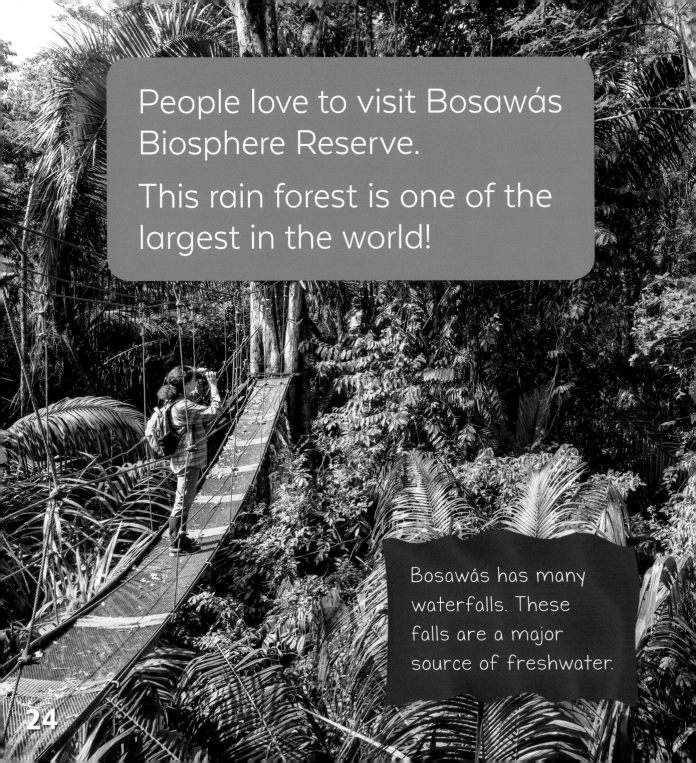

People love to visit Bosawás Biosphere Reserve.

This rain forest is one of the largest in the world!

Bosawás has many waterfalls. These falls are a major source of freshwater.

Monkeys, jaguars, and sloths live in the rain forest.

two-toed sloth

capuchin monkey

jaguar

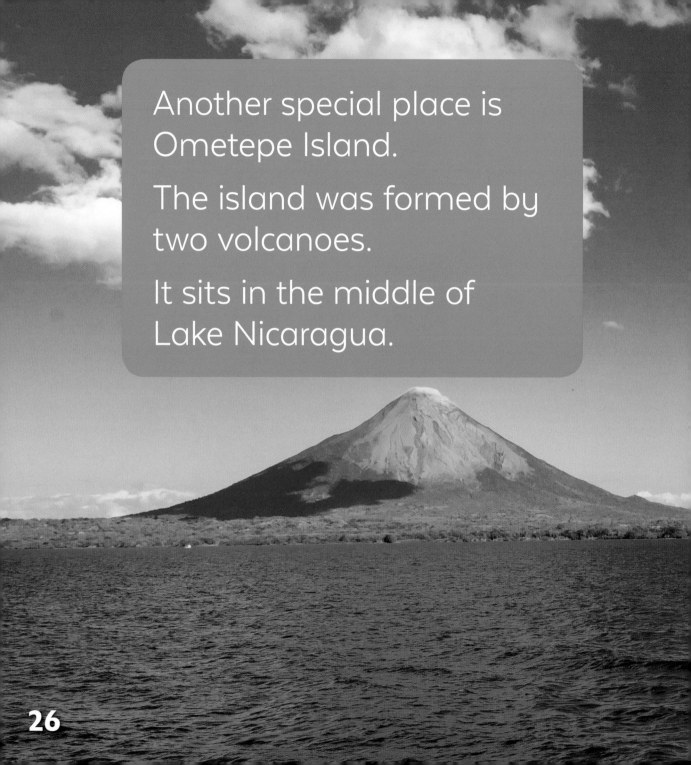

Another special place is Ometepe Island.

The island was formed by two volcanoes.

It sits in the middle of Lake Nicaragua.

Wild pigs look for food on Ometepe's many beaches.

27

Nicaragua has many festivals.

In October, people celebrate their **ancestors** during Los Agüizotes.

They dance, dress up like ghosts, and set off fireworks!

The San Lázaro festival celebrates dogs! It takes place in March.

Fast Facts

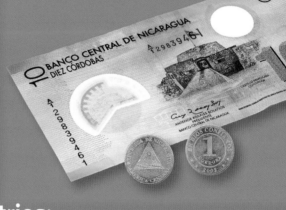

Capital city: Managua

Population of Nicaragua:
Over 6 million

Main language:
Spanish

Money: Córdoba

Major religion:
Roman Catholic

Neighboring countries:
Honduras and Costa Rica

Cool Fact: Lake Nicaragua is the largest lake in Central America. It has over 400 islands!

ancestors (AN-sess-turz) family members who lived a long time ago

capital (KAP-uh-tuhl) a city where a country's government is based

cathedrals (kuh-THEE-druhlz) large, important churches

lush (LUHSH) rich, healthy, and green

volcanoes (vol-KAY-nohz) openings in the earth's crust that allow ash and hot, melted rock to shoot out from deep inside

31

Index

Read More

Owings, Lisa. *Nicaragua (Blastoff! Readers: Exploring Countries).* New York: Scholastic (2014).

Torres, John A. *Meet Our New Student from Nicaragua.* Hallandale, FL: Mitchell Lane (2010).

Learn More Online

To learn more about Nicaragua, visit
www.bearportpublishing.com/CountriesWeComeFrom

About the Author

Sweetie Peason flies all over the world. She hasn't landed in Nicaragua yet, but just learning about the strange cloud forests there makes her want to visit.